LANGUAGE LEARNING
WORKBOOK

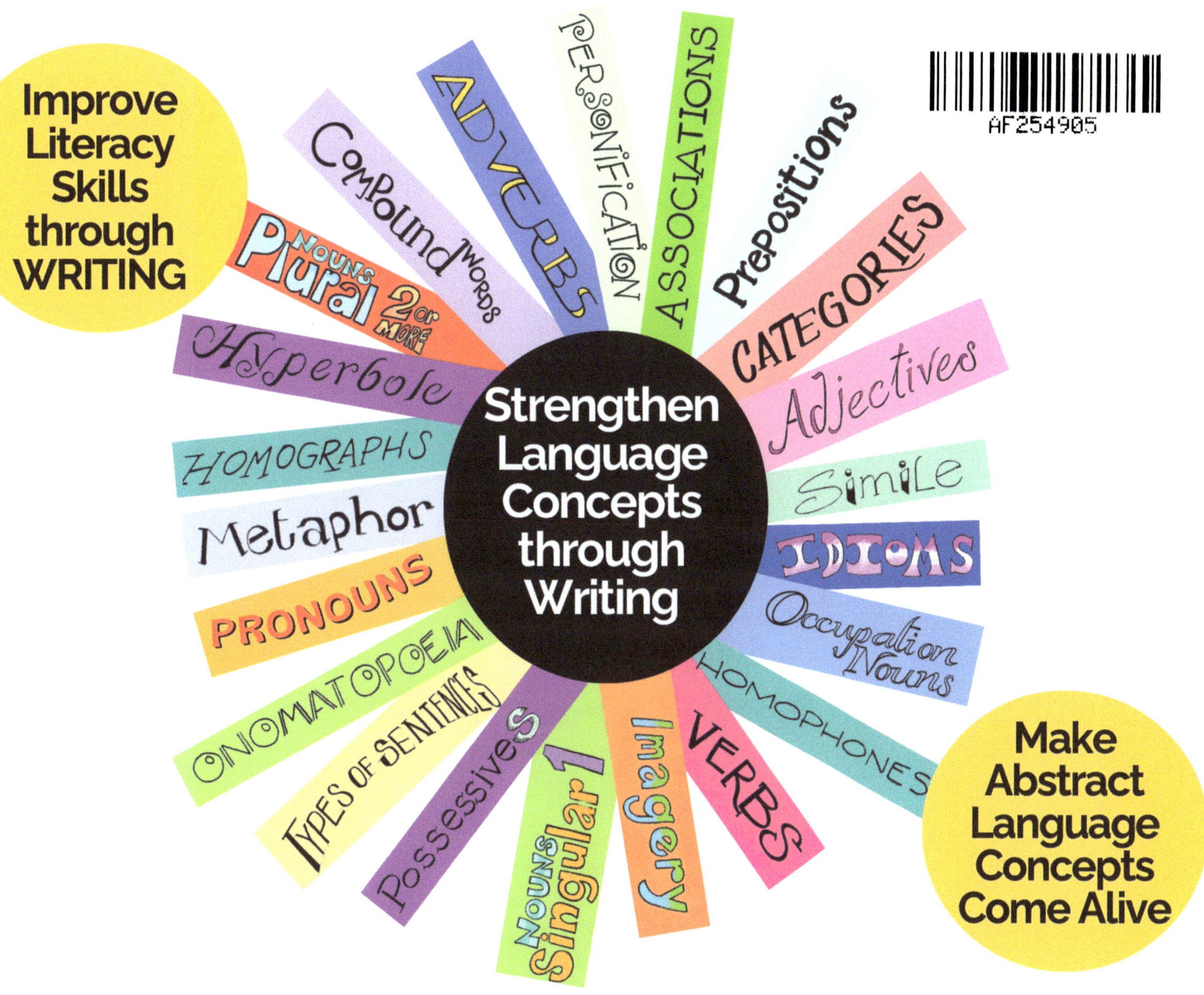

Created by ENID WEBB, MA
Illustrated by SHANE GUTHRIE

DEDICATION

I want to dedicate this work to my mom, who first ignited my love for literacy and language, and to my daughters, who are my greatest teachers and inspirations daily.

~ Enid

ACKNOWLEDGEMENTS

Shane, Thanks for being such a vital part of this project! You brought my vision to life, with your engaging artwork. Together, we created something truly meaningful, and I'm so grateful for your creativity and dedication.

Nikki, my gratitude for your friendship and support knows no bounds.

Linda, your editing, encouragement, and thoughtful feedback have made such a difference in this process.

Paul, your constant support and encouragement have been invaluable. Without you, I honestly don't know if I would have turned this book into a reality.

My students, I want to thank my extraordinary students. Your curiosity and enthusiasm have helped shape this workbook into something special. Your feedback has been incredibly helpful, and I truly appreciate the way we learn and grow together.

Mentors and Teachers: Mrs. Billings, Mrs. Hulsey, Mrs. Gladden, Mr. Sacco, Mr. Lipps, Mrs. Cannelora, Judith Brasseur, Judith Wells-Walberg, Brenda Moore, and Therese Bosshardt— a heartfelt thank you as you truly inspired and empowered me on my journey. As someone with multiple learning disabilities, I've faced my fair share of challenges, but you all have helped me defy the odds to get to where I am today. Your guidance and encouragement were invaluable. Your unwavering support fueled my passion for learning and language, making me believe that I can tackle any challenge that comes my way.

WHAT'S INSIDE
The Language Learning Workbook

Note from the Author, Book Overview, Foreword, Handwriting, Writing-Focused Approach, Syntax, Parts of Speech, Morphology, Semantics, Categorizing Information, Associations

TOPICS + WORKSHEETS

- ASSOCIATIONS
- COMPOUND WORDS
- CATEGORIES
- NOUNS
- Occupation Nouns
- VERBS
- PRONOUNS
- NOUNS Singular 1
- Plural NOUNS 2 or more
- Adjectives
- ADVERBS
- Possessives
- CONTRACTIONS
- Prepositions
- TYPES OF SENTENCES
- HOMOPHONES
- HOMOGRAPHS
- Simile
- Metaphor
- IDIOMS
- Hyperbole
- PERSONIFICATION
- Imagery
- ONOMATOPOEIA

NOTE FROM THE AUTHOR

My hope is that this book will make abstract language concepts more tangible and accessible through the use of illustrations.

Visual representations of complex ideas can be incredibly beneficial, especially for learners who may struggle with the theoretical aspects of language. By clarifying these concepts, we can make them easier to understand and remember, ultimately fostering strong literacy skills that encompass listening, speaking, reading, and writing.

While reading often garners the majority of attention within educational settings, it is essential to recognize that developing strong writing skills also significantly impacts overall literacy development. Writing is not merely a means of communication; it is an essential skill that reinforces reading comprehension and critical thinking. Research has shown that strong writing abilities can enhance all facets of literacy, as learners engage in the process of organizing their thoughts, analyzing information, and articulating their ideas effectively.

To support the importance of building language skills and writing for literacy development, numerous studies highlight the correlation between language proficiency and academic success. For instance, research indicates that students who receive comprehensive language instruction exhibit improved performance in reading and writing assessments. Moreover, effective writing instruction has been linked to greater engagement in academic tasks and increased motivation among students.

In conclusion, this book aims to provide educators/parents with the tools and insights necessary to foster strong language skills through structured literacy. By emphasizing the interconnectedness of language components and the importance of writing, we can empower students to become confident communicators and successful learners. I hope that you find this resource valuable in your journey to cultivate literacy skills in your students, ultimately helping them thrive in their academic pursuits and beyond.

BOOK OVERVIEW

This book has been thoughtfully created to systematically build and enhance strong language knowledge and skills through the principles of structured literacy.

This approach is rooted in a developmental hierarchical sequence of language, which is critical for nurturing robust literacy skills among learners.

Structured literacy instruction is not just a method; it is a philosophy grounded in the understanding that language acquisition is a cumulative process. By carefully and systematically developing strong language skills, educators have the unique opportunity to equip students with a solid foundation in literacy. This foundation will not only enhance their academic performance but will also serve them well beyond their school years, impacting their communication abilities and overall life success.

In this book, I have included essential language components that are critical to structured literacy. Each of these elements plays a significant role in fostering a comprehensive understanding of language:

1. Syntax: This refers to the study of sentence structure, word order, and grammar. Understanding syntax helps students construct coherent sentences and express their thoughts clearly.

2. Semantics: This component focuses on the meaning of words and how they relate to one another in various contexts. A strong grasp of semantics enables students to enhance their vocabulary and improve comprehension.

3. Morphology: This is the study of meaningful word parts, such as prefixes, suffixes, and root words. By understanding morphology, students can decipher unfamiliar words, thus expanding their language skills.

Additionally, I have included activities focusing on associations and categorization, because students learn to organize their language and make meaningful connections to their own experiences, they are more likely to retain information. This personalized approach to learning not only enhances memory but also fosters a deeper understanding of language concepts.

FOREWORD

By Linda Zeigler

This remarkable workbook, **Simple Effective Literacy Framework, takes the phrase, a picture is worth a thousand words, to a new level.** This adage suggests that a complex idea can be conveyed more effectively through an image than a mere description.

The author, Enid Webb and the illustrator, Shane Guthrie, recognized this truth and offer delightful imagery throughout the workbook to create conception for academic vocabulary. If students do not understand an abstract concept, they will not have an image.

These illustrations provide that image, moving each abstract term to a concrete concept. Terms like associations, categories, and imaging are identified, helping students organize thoughts while making an emotional connection to their real lives.

The captivating artwork provides a general category with examples for each word. Students then reflect and search the illustrations to clarify the concepts, discovering new examples and connecting each term to personal thinking. This learning process stimulates students to remember, understand, and apply each concept.

This book will serve as a powerful resource for teachers and parents with children of all ages.

When a new vocabulary word is identified, the pictures could be revisited and the new term could be easily organized into one or more of the conceptual terms.

(Linda Zeigler is a retired educator after 35 years in public schools in Kansas as an elementary teacher, reading teacher, principal, and superintendent of schools. She has also authored multiple books for teachers and is currently writing a series of children's books.)

Zeigler, Linda. (2026) Always Imaging Alice: Becoming a Thinker. Self-published, Amazon.

Zeigler, Linda. (2023) Piper's Picture Power: Becoming a Thinker. Self-published, Amazon.

Zeigler, Linda. (2022) Imagine Cognition using Intentional Visualization 2nd Edition. Self-published, Amazon.

Zeigler, L. L., Johns, J. L., & Beesley, V. R. (2007). Enhancing Writing through Visualization. Dubuque, Iowa: Kendall/Hunt.

Zeigler, L. L. & Johns, J. L. (2005). Visualization: Using Mental Images to Strengthen Comprehension. Dubuque, Iowa: Kendall/Hunt.

HANDWRITING

I have included handwriting pages throughout to emphasize the importance of handwriting practice in enhancing literacy skills and reducing cognitive load. Research shows that writing by hand can improve memory retention, comprehension, and overall learning. (Mueller & Oppenheimer, 2014)

Ultimately, these handwriting exercises are designed to foster a deeper connection to the learning process and promote academic success.

When discussing handwriting with older students, I often draw an analogy to familiar concepts to help them understand its importance. I explain that the lines on a page are much like the boundaries of a go-kart track. Just as the track keeps the go-kart on course, the lines in handwriting provide the necessary parameters that help maintain form and structure.

Imagine zooming around a go-kart track without any boundaries; it would be easy to veer off course, leading to chaos and confusion. Similarly, when we write, those lined boundaries serve as guides, ensuring that each letter is formed correctly and that words are neatly organized.

By staying within the lines, we can create clear and legible handwriting, just as a go-kart driver stays on the track to navigate effectively. These parameters not only help us maintain consistency but also enhance the readability of our writing, making it more understandable for others.

I encourage my students to see handwriting not just as a chore, but as a skill that requires practice and attention to detail—just like mastering a go-kart track. With patience and perseverance, they can learn to navigate their own writing journey successfully!

WRITING-FOCUSED APPROACH

Writing is a fundamental skill that plays a critical role in communication, learning, and personal expression.

Focused instruction in writing not only enhances the ability to articulate thoughts and ideas but also brings a variety of cognitive and academic benefits.

One of the most significant advantages of writing by hand is its positive impact on memory retention and understanding. Research indicates that handwriting engages different cognitive processes compared to typing, leading to better encoding of information. When students write by hand, they are more likely to synthesize information, facilitating deeper comprehension and retention of material. This practice can improve reading comprehension, as students who engage in handwriting often gain a better grasp of the text, enabling them to summarize and analyze content more effectively.

Additionally, writing by hand can enhance reading fluency. The physical act of writing helps reinforce the recognition of words and phrases, making it easier for students to read with speed and accuracy. This connection between writing and reading fluency underscores the importance of integrated literacy instruction, where writing activities complement reading exercises.

Moreover, focused writing instruction fosters improvement in overall writing skills. Regular practice helps students develop their voice, structure, and style, leading to more coherent and compelling written work. When students receive targeted feedback on their writing, they learn to revise and refine their ideas, contributing to their growth as proficient writers.

In summary, writing is essential not only for effective communication, but also for enhancing cognitive development and academic achievement. Benefits such as improved reading comprehension, increased reading fluency, and stronger writing skills underscore the importance of incorporating focused writing instruction into educational curricula. By emphasizing the value of writing, educators can equip students with the tools necessary for success in their academic and personal lives.

SYNTAX/PARTS OF SPEECH

The significance of grammar/syntax/parts of speech:

Grammar, syntax, and the various parts of speech—such as nouns, verbs, adjectives, and adverbs—are essential components of effective communication. Each part of speech plays a distinct role within a sentence, and understanding these roles is vital for both reading and writing. Recognizing how different parts of speech fit together enhances clarity and coherence in communication.

Developing a strong foundation in parts of speech is crucial for mastering language structure and meaning. For writers, this knowledge enables the construction of clear and effective sentences, ultimately improving overall communication. By understanding how parts of speech interact, writers can create engaging content that conveys their intended message.

For readers, identifying parts of speech is an invaluable skill that aids in deciphering complex sentences. It helps in understanding the relationships between ideas, revealing the overall message of the text. This understanding is particularly important when encountering intricate or nuanced writing.

Furthermore, grasping how different parts of speech function provides a pathway for learning new vocabulary and using words correctly in various contexts. For instance, knowing that adding the suffix -ous transforms a noun into an adjective enhances both spelling and understanding of language.

A strong command of parts of speech serves as a foundation for mastering grammar rules, which is essential for both writing and comprehending texts. This knowledge not only enhances reading comprehension but also strengthens writing skills and overall communication effectiveness.

Syntax skills included in this workbook: Common nouns, proper nouns, plural nouns, pronouns, verbs and verb tenses, adjectives, adverbs, prepositions, and possessive forms.

MORPHOLOGY

Morphology is the study of the structure and formation of words in a language.

It involves analyzing the smallest units of meaning, known as morphemes, which can be roots, prefixes, suffixes, or inflections. Understanding morphology is crucial for spelling because it helps individuals recognize how words are constructed and how their meanings can change with different morphological components.

When an affix is added to the front of a word, a prefix, or to the back of the word, a suffix, the meaning and mental image for the root word changes.

Common **suffixes,** such as -ing or -ed assist in forming and spelling different verb tenses, changing the part of speech, conjunction, or other grammatical properties of a word. Understanding that when a suffix is added to the end of a word, the meaning and mental image for the root word changes; consider smile, smiling, and smiled.

Smile is the base form of the verb.
Smiling is present tense, happening now or ongoing.
Smiled is past tense, happened in the past.
Will smile or -is going to smile is future tense, happening in the future.

Plural suffixes, such as s, es, ies, indicate that there are more than one, changing the number of things that are imaged. Examples of root word and that plural nouns follow:

book - books
peach - peaches
candy - candies
elf-elves

Overall, a strong grasp of morphology enhances spelling skills, vocabulary development, and reading comprehension by promoting an understanding of the relationships between words and their meanings.

Morphology skills included in this workbook: Plural, possessive, and verb tense suffixes.

SEMANTICS

Semantic development is a key part of literacy and communication, playing an essential role in a child's education and everyday life.

Literacy goes beyond just reading and writing; it's about effective communication too. When kids develop their semantic skills, they learn to express their thoughts clearly and engage in conversations, which is crucial for collaborative learning.

A strong vocabulary is vital for understanding texts and expressing ideas. The more words children know, the better they read and write. Plus, semantic development encourages critical thinking about language, helping kids analyze texts, draw conclusions, and make inferences—important skills for literacy.

As kids improve their semantic skills, they become better at figuring out meaning from context, which aids in understanding complex texts. It also helps them grasp story structures, including themes, character development, and plots, which is key for reading comprehension and writing narratives.

Good semantic skills are linked to success in academics across all subjects. A solid vocabulary is foundational for learning, and students who struggle with semantics often find reading and writing challenging, impacting their overall performance.

Language is also tied to culture. By developing semantic skills, children learn about cultural references and idiomatic expressions, making it easier for them to connect with diverse people and texts.

Encouraging semantic development early on can significantly boost a child's literacy skills and enrich their overall educational journey.

Semantic concepts included in this workbook: Homophones, homographs, simile, metaphor, onomatopoeia, personification, hyperbole, idioms, and imagery.

CATEORIZING INFORMATION

Categorizing information is an essential skill for learning and life:

- Organizing information into categories helps students better understand and internalize complex concepts.

- It breaks down large amounts of information into manageable parts, making it easier to grasp.

- Information that is categorized is easier to remember. When students group related information together, they create mental connections that aid in recall.

- Categorization encourages students to analyze and evaluate information, allowing them to identify similarities, differences, and relationships between concepts. This critical thinking process is vital for deeper thinking.

- Learning how to categorize information helps students develop organizational skills that are beneficial not only in academic settings but also in everyday life and future workplaces.

- Categorization facilitates connections between different subjects or topics, fostering a more integrated understanding of their learning and promoting interdisciplinary thinking.

- Categorizing information helps students plan and express their ideas more clearly and coherently by providing a framework for organizing thoughts. This is essential for writing essays, giving presentations, and engaging in discussions.

The ability to categorize information is fundamental for effective learning, critical thinking, and overall academic success. It equips students with tools that are applicable across various domains of knowledge and life skills.

ASSOCIATIONS

Associations help learners connect new information to existing knowledge:

- Improve Recall: When learners create associations, they build mental networks that make it easier to retrieve information from memory, enhancing recall during assessments or discussions.

- Support Critical Thinking: By linking new information to existing knowledge, learners can analyze and evaluate ideas more critically, fostering higher-order thinking skills.

- Encourage Active Learning: Creating associations requires active engagement with the material, promoting an interactive learning experience that enhances retention.

- Aid in Problem Solving: Associations help learners draw parallels between different concepts, allowing them to apply knowledge creatively to solve problems in innovative ways.

- Strengthen Neural Connections: The process of forming associations strengthens neural pathways in the brain, making it easier to access and utilize information in the future.

- Boost Motivation and Interest: By finding personal relevance in the material through associations, learners are more likely to feel motivated, engaged, and invested in their learning journey.

- Enhance Collaboration: When learners share their associations with peers, they can gain new perspectives and insights, enriching the learning experience through collaborative discussions.

- Make Learning Holistic: Understanding associations allows learners to see the big picture, integrating various concepts into a cohesive framework that supports overall comprehension.

Associations play a critical role in how we process, retain, and apply knowledge, making them both fundamental and essential to effective learning.

· ASSOCIATIONS ·

TWO PEAS IN A POD

PEANUT BUTTER
AND JELLY

HOT DOGS AND BUNS

LET'S PLAY WITH ASSOCIATIONS!

Start with a common word (e.g., peas, hot dog) then, the choose another word that relates to that word (e.g., pod, bun).

Write your own word associations using the words below.

Example:

Hot Dog >>> Bun >>> Picnic >>> Park >>> Swings >>> Carnival >>> Rides >>> Roller Coaster >>> Amusement Park>>> ?

>>>

>>>

>>>

>>>

>>>

ASSOCIATIONS

Word association are a fun way to expand vocabulary
and improve recall and memory abilities.

Now write some of your own!

Example: snow   sledding

cat _______________________________

pepper _______________________________

rain _______________________________

ocean _______________________________

wheels _______________________________

pencil _______________________________

jungle _______________________________

summer _______________________________

pizza _______________________________

Compound Words

2, or more words

Combined to make...

1 Word

CUPCAKE   BUTTERFLY

Compound Words

Write compound words using this list of words.

base	rain	blue	sun
horse	pan	fish	ball
tooth	bow	berry	flower
cake	shoe	star	brush

Examples:

base + ball = baseball   pan + cake = pancake

CATEGORIES

Things, objects, and creatures found in the Ocean.

List the objects/items/nouns you found in the picture.

EXAMPLE: Seaweed

CATEGORIES

Name the categories you see in the picture.

1. Sadness, surprise, happiness: Emotions

2. Race car, bike, skates: Things with wheels

Apples, oranges, grapes: _______________________

Chair, table, couch: _______________________

Jaguar, monkey, elephant:_______________________

Ring, bracelet, necklace: _______________________

Wrench, hammer, drill: _______________________

Pen, paint, pencil: _______________________

June, July, August:_______________________

Daisy, rose, tulip: _______________________

Ladybug, beetle, fly: _______________________

freedom hope love dreams joy friendship
LOVE
HOPE
JOY
DREAMS
J. Guthrie

IDEAS/

Write idea nouns below from the picture.
Then write some more of your own.

Example: _______freedom_______

Occupation
Nouns
TEAM
Nouns
MOM
Nouns 4 Life
NOUNS SPEED WAY
11
TEAM WER-3AX
N

Occupation Nouns
People Nouns

Find the occupations/people in the picture and write them below. Then write some of your own.

Example: Magician

PLACES/ 

List the places you go to or wish to go.

Example: Disneyland, zoo, school

PROPER AND COMMON

Proper Nouns

Specific Names
Capitalized
Days of the Week
States, Counties, Cities
Specific Names: Natalie, Craig, Grace

Common Nouns

General Names
Not Capitalized
General places: school, airport, park
Things and Ideas
General People: man, teacher, dancer

Write your own proper and common nouns below.
Remember to capitalize proper nouns.

PROPER AND COMMON

Write your own proper and common nouns below.
Remember to capitalize proper nouns.

Proper Nouns

Specific Names

Common Nouns

General Names

PROPER 

IN SENTENCES

Write sentences using the proper nouns you chose.

Capitalization: Capitalize the first word and any proper nouns in your sentences.

BOARD WALK
VERBS

ACTIONS

VERBS
ACTION VERBS

Write as many action verbs as you can from the beach action picture.

Write a few of your own favorite action verbs.

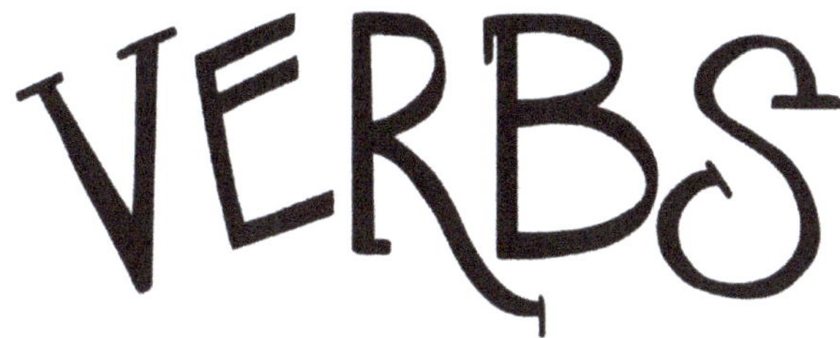 VERBS

Action Verbs

Jump   Show   Split   Write
Run   Ask   Snap   Carry
Play   Smile   Fly   Hide
Eat   Laugh   Talk   Draw

Helping Verbs

Be, being, been, is, am, are, was were, has, have, had, can could, shall, should, will, would, may, might, must, do, did, does

Write sentences with any of the verbs listed above.

Action Verbs

Skip	Slide	Walk	Take
Throw	Make	Plant	Drink
Catch	Chew	Play	Sweep
Feed	Swim	Ride	Pitch

Helping Verbs

Be, being, been, is, am, are, was were, has, have, had, can could, shall, should, will, would, may, might, must, do, did, does

Write sentences with any of the verbs listed above.

VERB TENSES

Fill in the past, present, and future tense forms of the verbs.

PAST TENSE Yesterday/Before	PRESENT TENSE Today/Now	FUTURE TENSE Tomorrow/Later
Played	Playing/Plays	Will play
Planted	Planting /Plants	Going to plant
Tripped	Tripping/Trip	Will trip
Ate	Eating/Eats	Going to eat
	Clapping	
	Smile	
	Clean	
	Write	

VERB TENSES

PAST TENSE Yesterday/Before	**PRESENT TENSE** Today/Now	**FUTURE TENSE** Tomorrow/Later

PAST TENSE VERBS

Write sentences using past tense verbs from the list
you generated on the previous page.

FUTURE TENSE VERBS

Write sentences using future tense verbs
from the list you generated.

PRONOUNS

A WORD THAT REPLACES A NOUN.

She   Tasha has a big heart.

It   The tree is big.

They   John and Vee are on a trip.

EXAMPLES: I, you, he, she, it, we, they, me, you, him, her, us, them.

Replace nouns with pronouns in the following sentences.

The boat belongs to Mary.

The girls are playing a game.

Replace nouns with pronouns in the following sentences.

The food is scrumptious.

Nikki and Gerry are hilarious.

Paul is a great snowboarder.

NOUNS Singular 1

1 FOX

1 ELF

1 PUPPY

1 BALLOON

NOUNS Plural 2 or MORE

2 FOXES

2 ELVES

2 PUPPIES

2 BALLOONS

List as many plural nouns as you can.
If you get stuck, try finding things around you.

Example: Socks

When we want to make a word plural (more than one) that ends in y, we often change the y to an i and add es.

Exception: When there is a vowel before the y, we only add an s.. Examples : days, turkeys, boys

Change these words into the plural form.

Example: Baby  **Babies**

Family 

Lady 

City 

Candy 

Try 

Cry 

Fly 

When we want to make a word plural (more than one) that ends in **f**, we change the **f** to a **v** and add **es**.

Change these words into the plural form.

Example: Wolf → **Wolves**

Elf →

Shelf →

Half →

Calf →

Life →

Knife →

Loaf →

Adjectives
WORDS THAT DESCRIBE A NOUN OR PRONOUN
COLORFUL
BIG
LOVELY
SHY
SCARED
VIBRANT
STRONG
UNIQUE
FAST
Peacock
Noun

Adjectives

Adjectives are single words that describe nouns and pronouns.

Write the adjectives from the previous picture that describe the peacock on the lines below.

Peacock (common noun)

Adjectives

Choose a food item to describe with adjectives.
Use your senses to help you describe.

Describe a food item below.
How does it look (e.g., small, round, color)?
How does it feel (e.g., soft, smooth, rough, bumpy)?
How does it smell (e.g., salty, sweet)?
How does it taste (e.g., yummy, delicious)?

Food Item _________________________ **(common noun)**

We use adjectives to describe characters in stories. We can also use adjectives to describe ourselves and our loved ones.

Describe yourself or another person below.

Name of Person________________ (proper noun)

_______________________   _______________________

_______________________   _______________________

_______________________   _______________________

_______________________   _______________________

_______________________   _______________________

_______________________   _______________________

 ADVERBS

Words that modify/describe verbs,
adjectives or other adverbs.

WHEN ?

She always arrives early.
(adverb) (verb)

HOW?

He runs fast.
(verb) (adverb)

WHERE?

The children play outside.
(verb) (adverb)

IN WHAT WAY

She eats slowly.
(verb) (adverb)

TO WHAT EXTENT

My cat is incredibly happy to be eating
his dinner. (adverb) (adjective)

ADVERBS
MY CAT IS INCREDIBLY HAPPY TO BE HAVING HIS DINNER
"IS MY SINGING TOO LOUD?" ASKED SHANE.

ADVERBS

ADVERBS

Use one of the following adverbs to write
sentences of your own:

always, fast, outside, incredibly, carefully,

Use one of the following adverbs to write
more sentences of your own:

everywhere, today, tomorrow, loudly, slowly

Possessive S

CRAIG'S SMILE

SHANE'S SKATEBOARD

NATALIE'S CAT

GRACE'S DOG

Possessive S 

The possessive form shows that something belongs to someone or something. To make a word possessive, we just add an apostrophe and an "s" at the end.

For example, if you have a toy that belongs to your friend, you could say "my friend's toy." That apostrophe and "s" tell us that the toy is owned by your friend.

Finish the sentences.

EXAMPLE: Craig's smile *is as beautiful as a sunset.*

Shane's skateboard

Natalie's cat

Grace's dog

Possessive S

Finish the sentences.

The family's car

The dog's bone

The cat's

Mom's

iS + not = iSn't

Contractions are when two words become one word.

An apostrophe will fill the space of the missing letters.

I + am = I'm

we + are = we're

she + will = she'll

he + is = he's

do + not = don't

you + have = you've

it + is = it's

did + not = didn't

you + would = you'd

they + are = they're

While writing with contractions is more informal and not encouraged in formal writing, it is important to be able to quickly decipher them when reading.

Write sentences with the contractions from the previous page.

Prepositions

above • between • behind
below • in front • next to

in • on

PrePositions

Prepositions

Prepositions are words that show the relationship between a noun or pronoun and other words in a sentence, often indicating direction, location, time, or manner (e.g., in, on, at, under, before).

Write sentences with the following prepositions:
above, between, behind, below

Prepositions

Prepositions are words that show the relationship between a noun or pronoun and other words in a sentence, often indicating direction, location, time, or manner (e.g., in, on, at, under, before).

Write sentences using the following prepositions:
in, on, under, beside

Types of Sentences

- **DECLARATIVE** – a statement
  I have a cat named Whiskers.
  I just started playing the piano.

- **INTERROGATIVE** – a question
  Does Whiskers like me?
  How long will it be before I'm playing Beethoven?

- **EXCLAMATORY** – an exclamation
  Ouch, that hurt, Whiskers!
  Piano lessons went great!

- **IMPERATIVE** – a command or request
  Leave Whiskers alone!
  Listen to what I learned on the Piano.

Using examples, write your own sentences.

Declarative Sentence:
Telling about a statement.

Interrogative Sentence:
A question.

Exclamatory Sentence:

An exclamation.

Imparative Sentence:

A command or request.

HOMOPHONES

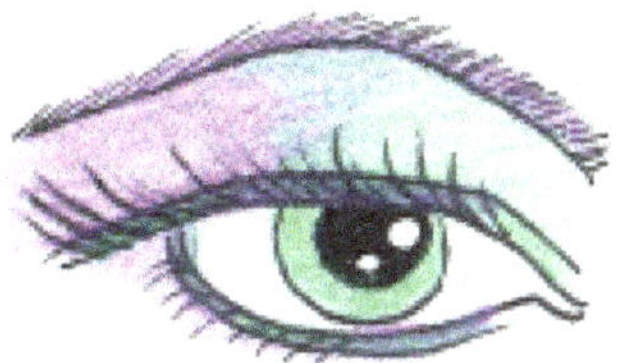

SEE

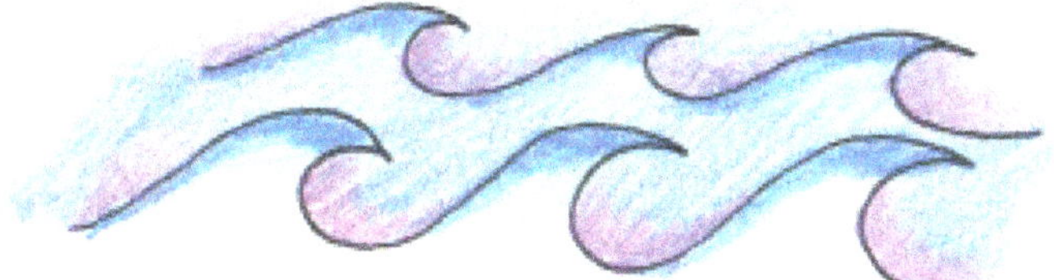

SEA

WHOLE

HOLE

PEAK

PEEK

HOMOPHONES

Homophones are words that sound the same but have different meanings and often different spellings.

Write sentences with the following homophones.

Buy/By

Sea/See

HOMOPHONES

Homophones are words that sound the same but have different meanings and often different spelling.

Write sentences with the following homophones.

Rode/Road

Hole/Whole

HOMOGRAPHS

HOMOGRAPHS

Homographs are two or more words spelled the same but not necessarily pronounced the same and have different meanings and origins.

Use these words to write two sentences each.

Bat

Fly

HOMOGRAPHS

Homographs are two or more words spelled the same but not necessarily pronounced the same and have different meanings and origins.

Use these words to write two sentences each.

Match

Read (present and past tense)

Simile

When you compare two things using the words "like" or "as".

Example: Grandpa is as wise as an owl

Examples of Simile

These similes enhance language and writing by making comparisons that evoke vivid imagery or convey specific qualities.

As brave as a lion
Meaning: Very courageous; showing great bravery.

As busy as a bee
Meaning: Very active and industrious; working hard.

As cool as a cucumber
Meaning: Very calm and composed, especially in stressful situations.

As old as the hills
Meaning: Very old; ancient.

As clear as mud
Meaning: Very unclear or confusing.

As light as a feather
Meaning: Very light in weight; easy to carry or lift.

Simile

Write sentences using the examples from the previous page or some of your own.

Metaphor

When you compare two things not using "like" or "as"

Comparing two things using "is" or "was"

He is a bear

Examples of Metaphor

These metaphors enhance language by creating vivid imagery and conveying deeper meanings beyond the literal interpretation.

Time is a thief.

Meaning: Time can stealthily take away moments from our lives, similar to how a thief steals possessions.

The world is a stage.

Meaning: Life is like a theatre where people play different roles, suggesting that we often act rather than being our true selves.

He's a lion in battle.

Meaning: He is very brave and courageous, likening his qualities to those of a lion, which is often seen as a symbol of strength and bravery.

Her voice is music to my ears.

Meaning: Her voice is very pleasant or enjoyable to listen to, akin to the joy one receives from music.

He has a heart of stone.

Meaning: He is emotionally unresponsive or unfeeling, suggesting a lack of compassion or empathy.

The classroom was a zoo.

Meaning: The classroom was chaotic or disorderly, comparing it to a zoo where animals are often wild and noisy.

Life is a journey.

Meaning: Life involves various experiences and phases, similar to traveling along a path with different destinations and obstacles.

Metaphor

Write sentences using the examples from the previous page or some of your own.

IDIOMS

She has butterflies in her stomach

She is nervous.

Examples of Idioms

Break the ice
To initiate conversation in a social setting, making people feel more comfortable.

Bite the bullet
To face a difficult or unpleasant situation with courage.

Burn the midnight oil
To work late into the night.

Hit the nail on the head
To describe exactly what is causing a situation or problem.

Let the cat out of the bag
To reveal a secret or disclose information inadvertently.

Write sentences using the idioms from the previous page or some of your own.

Hyperbole

When you exaggerate.

Example: He ran faster than the wind.

Examples of *Hyperbole*

Hyperbole creates emphasis, evokes strong emotions, and adds humor or drama to language.

I'm so hungry I could eat a horse.
Meaning: The speaker is extremely hungry, but not literally capable of eating a horse.

I've told you a million times.
Meaning: The speaker has repeated something many times, not literally a million.

It was so cold, I saw polar bears wearing jackets.
Meaning: It was very cold, to the point of absurdity.

This bag weighs a ton!
Meaning: The bag is very heavy, but it does not literally weigh a ton.

I'm dying of embarrassment.
Meaning: The speaker feels extremely embarrassed, but is not literally dying.

Hyperbole

Write sentences with the hyperbole examples from the previous page or some of your own.

PERSONiFiCATiON

WHEN YOU MAKE THINGS LOOK OR ACT LIKE A HUMAN.

Examples of PERSONIFICATION

These examples illustrate how personification attributes human/animal qualities to non-human/animal entities, enhancing imagery and emotional connection.

The wind whispered through the trees.
Meaning: The wind is given the human ability to whisper, suggesting a gentle and calming presence.

Time flies when you're having fun.
Meaning: Time is depicted as if it can fly, implying that enjoyable moments seem to pass quickly.

The sun smiled down on us.
Meaning: The sun is described as smiling, conveying warmth and happiness on a bright day.

The flowers danced in the breeze.
Meaning: Flowers are portrayed as dancing, suggesting they are lively and animated in the gentle wind.

Fear crept into my heart.
Meaning: Fear is characterized as something that can creep, indicating it can invade one's emotions subtly and unexpectedly.

PERSONIFICATION

Write sentences with the personification examples from the previous page or some of your own.

Imagery

WHEN YOU USE DESCRIPTIVE WORDS TO PAINT A PICTURE IN THE READER'S HEAD.

Examples of *Imagery*

Imagery enhances writing by creating vivid mental pictures that engage the senses, allowing readers to experience the emotions and scenes more deeply. It helps to evoke feelings, set the mood, and immerse the audience in the narrative.

Walking with His Dog

The boy trudged through the sun-dappled park, his sneakers crunching on the gravel path while his beloved dog trotted beside him; its fluffy tail wagging , and catching the afternoon light.

Flying with His Dog

As the boy soared through the sky, the wind whipped through his hair, and the dog's ears flapped joyfully like banners in the breeze; both of them sharing a triumphant laugh as they danced among the clouds.

Dog Chewing on a Bone

In the cozy corner of the living room, the dog lay sprawled on a sun-warmed rug, gnawing diligently on a marrow bone; the rhythmic crunching echoing softly as bits flew like confetti in the air.

Imagery

Write about the boy and his dog or something you choose. Include as many details as possible to help the reader picture/imagine what you are thinking.

ONOMATOPOEIA

WHEN YOU USE WORDS THAT MAKE A SOUND.

Examples of ONOMATOPOEIA

Onomatopoeia adds auditory elements to the text, helping readers visualize and hear the scenes being described.

Buzz

As the summer afternoon wore on, the air was filled with the buzz of bees flitting from flower to flower.

Whack

As he swung the bat, there was a satisfying whack as the ball soared into the sky.

Tweet

Early in the morning, I woke up to the cheerful tweet of birds outside my window.

Dingdong

The doorbell rang with a cheerful dingdong, announcing the arrival of our guests.

ONOMATOPOEIA

Write sentences, using the onomatopoeia/sound words from the previous page or choose your own.

FINISH

CONNECT WITH US!

About the Author, Enid Webb, M.A.

Enid Webb is a dedicated literacy specialist and interventionist with a Master's degree in Speech Pathology and Audiology. With a robust foundation in speech-language pathology, Enid began her career in the educational sector, where she worked as a speech-language pathologist in schools. Her experience spans co-teaching structured literacy across all grade levels, from kindergarten through high school, and providing training to kindergarten and reading teachers on effective structured literacy practices.

Throughout her career, Enid has served as the Response to Intervention (RTI) facilitator for her district and as an assistive technology evaluator, roles that have enriched her understanding of the diverse needs of students. Drawing on this extensive experience, she founded Silver Lining Education Services, where she specializes in delivering targeted, data-driven structured literacy instruction with a particular emphasis on language development and writing.

Enid's commitment to advancing literacy skills in students is evident in both her teaching and her ongoing research efforts, making her a valuable resource in literacy education.

About the Illustrator, Shane Guthrie

From a young age, Shane exhibited a passion for art, finding inspiration in the simple tools of pencil and paper. As a child, he envisioned his creations, skillfully capturing the interplay of light and shadow. During kindergarten, he viewed the classroom as his canvas, eagerly producing artworks to present to his parents.

Throughout his educationl, Shane diligently pursued every available art class. His dedication culminated in receiving a scholarship to the Fashion Institute of Design & Merchandising (FIDM).

Shane has created large murals and self-portraits, often assisting friends with their artistic ideas, demonstrating an unwavering commitment to fostering creativity. Collaborating on this project with Enid has been a rewarding artistic experience. Shane eagerly anticipates future projects and hopes this book will positively impact every child who uses it.

www.silverliningsed.com   **email: silverliningsed@gmail.com**

REFERENCES

Bowers, A. A., & Cooke, K. (2012). The Effects of Morphological Instruction on Vocabulary and Comprehension. Reading and Writing, 25 (2), 453-472.

Catts, H. W., & Kamhi, A. G. (2014). Language and Reading Disabilities.Pearson.

Carlisle, J. F. (2010). Morphological Awareness and Early Literacy. Learning Disabilities Research & Practice, 25 (1), 40-50.

Eysenck, M. W., & Keane, M. T. (2015). Cognitive Psychology: A Student's Handbook. Psychology Press.

Fitzgerald, J., & Shanahan, T. (2000). Reading and Writing Relations and Their Development. Educational Psychologist, 35(1), 39-50.

Gentry, J. R. (2005). The Science of Reading: A Handbook. The New England Reading Association Journal, 41(1), 16-22.

Graham, S. (2018). Effective Writing Instruction. The Reading Teacher, 72(3), 243-247.

Graham, S., & Perin, D. (2007). A Meta-Analysis of the Effectiveness of Writing Instruction for Students in Elementary and Middle School. Educational Psychologist, 42(4), 245-265.

Harris, K. R., & Graham, S. (2010). Self-Regulated Strategy Development: A Comprehensive Model for Writing Instruction. In Handbook of Writing Research (pp. 158-171). New York: Guilford Press.

Kelley, M. J., & Clausen-Grace, N. (2010). Writing to Read: Evidence for How Writing Can Improve Reading. The Reading Teacher, 64(1), 12-23.

Kelley, P. (2013). The Importance of Semantic Knowledge in Literacy Development. The Reading Teacher, 66*(5), 370-373.

Langer, J. A. (2001). Becoming a Writer: A Study of the Impact of Writing Instruction on Literacy Development. The Elementary School Journal, 102(2), 183-196.

Moats, L. C. (2010). Speech to Print: Language Essentials for Teachers. Brookes Publishing.

National Writing Project. (2010). Because Writing Matters: Improving Student Writing in Our Schools.

Nagy, W. E., & Anderson, R. C. (1984). How Many Words Are There in Printed School English? Reading Research Quarterly, 19(3), 304-330.

Rosch, E. (1978). Principles of Categorization. In Cognition and Categorization (p. 27-48). Hillsdale, NJ: Lawrence Erlbaum Associates.

Smith, E. E., & Medin, D. L. (1981). Categories and Concepts. Cambridge, MA: Harvard University Press.

Vaughn, S., & Linan-Thompson, S. (2003). Response to Intervention as a Means of Identifying Students with Reading/Language Disabilities. Learning Disabilities Research & Practice, 18(3), 119-125.

9 781953 978370